Earth Science

Anita Ganeri

Evans Brothers Limited

Published by Evans Brothers Limited
2A Portman Mansions
Chiltern Street
London W1M 1LE

© text Anita Ganeri 1993
© illustrations Evans Brothers Limited 1993

First published 1993
Reprinted 1997, 1998, 1999

All Rights Reserved.
No part of this publication may be reproduced, stored in a retrieval system
or transmitted in any form or by any means, electronic, mechanical,
photocopying, recording or otherwise, without prior permission
of Evans Brothers Limited.

Printed in Hong Kong

ISBN 0 237 51247 5

Acknowledgements

The author and publishers would like to thank the following
for her valuable help and advice:
Nicky Tovey BA MA

Illustrations: Virginia Gray – pages 8, 10, 12, 14, 23, 24, 25, 26, 34, 40, 43, 44
Jillian Luff of Bitmap Graphics – pages 9, 13, 32
Editors: Catherine Chambers and Jean Coppendale
Design: Monica Chia

For permission to reproduce copyright material the author
and publishers gratefully acknowledge the following:
Cover photographs: (main picture) The Earth photographed from Space, Frank Lane Picture Agency; (top left) Volcanco, Hawaii, Planet Earth Pictures; (bottom left) Coral Sea, the Red Sea, Robert Harding Picture Library; (bottom right) Sahara sand-dunes, Robert Harding Picture Library.
Page 6 - (bottom) Soames Summerhays, Biofotos; page 8 - (top) Sally Bensusen, Science Photo Library, (bottom) Mary Evans Picture Library; page 9 - FLPA; page 10 - Jeff Foott Productions, Bruce Coleman Limited; page 11 - (bottom left) Robert Harding Picture Library, (middle right) John Lythgoe, Planet Earth Pictures; page 13 - (top) SIPA-PRESS, (inset) David E Rowley; page 14 - (right) Dorian Weisel, Planet Earth Pictures; page 15 - (bottom left) Sally Morgan, Ecoscene, (bottom right) A.N.T., NHPA; page 16 - (bottom left) P A Hinchliffe, Bruce Coleman Limited, (bottom right) John Eastcott, Planet Earth Pictures, (inset) Vincent Serventy, Planet Earth Pictures; page 17 - (top) Ken Lucas, Planet Earth Pictures, (bottom left) Anthony King, (bottom right) Anthony King; page 18 - (middle) John Mead, Science Photo Library, (bottom right) Ken Lucas, Planet Earth Pictures, (inset) Hutchison Library; page 19 - (top) James Holmes, Science Photo Library, (bottom) Alex Bartel, Science Photo Library; page 20 - (bottom) Jim Amos, Science Photo Library, (inset) Ken Lucas, Planet Earth Pictures; page 21 - (top) Ken Vaughn; Planet Earth Pictures, (bottom) Sally Morgan, Ecoscene; page 22 - (bottom) Heather Angel, (inset left) David Woodfall, NHPA, (inset right) David Woodfall, NHPA; page 23 - Paul Trummer, The Image Bank; page 24 - (top) C C Lockwood, Earth Scenes, Oxford Scientific Films, (bottom) John Downer, Planet Earth Pictures; page 26 - (bottom left) Ronald Goulds, Bruce Coleman Limited, (bottom right) David Woodfall, NHPA; page 27 - Dr Eckart Pott, Bruce Coleman Limited; page 28 - (bottom) Gerald Cubitt, Bruce Coleman Limited, (inset) Chris Howes, Planet Earth Pictures; page 29 - (bottom left) William M Smithey Jr., Planet Earth Pictures, (bottom right) Sally Morgan, Ecoscene; page 30 - (bottom left) Wayne Lankinen, Bruce Coleman Limited, (inset) Patti Murray, Oxford Scientific Films; page 31 - (top) Anthony King, (bottom) Wilkinson, Ecoscene; page 33 - (top) Oxford Scientific Films, (inset) Peter Parks, Oxford Scientific Films; page 34 - Don James, Zefa; page 35 - (left) Gryniewicz, Ecoscene, (right) Gryniewicz, Ecoscene; page 36 - (middle) Flip Schuike, Planet Earth Pictures, (inset) Romilly Lockyer, The Image Bank; page 37 - John Lythgoe, Planet Earth Pictures; page 38 - (middle) Kevin Aitken, NHPA, (left inset) Peter Parks, Oxford Scientific Films, (right inset) Christian Petron, Planet Earth Pictures; page 39 - (top) Peter Hendrie, The Image Bank, (middle) Michael Glover, Bruce Coleman Limited, (inset) Whittle, Ecoscene; page 41 - H Reinhard, Zefa; page 42 - (bottom) Joe Szkodinski, The Image Bank, (inset) Eyal Bartov, Oxford Scientific Films; page 43 - Ian Griffiths, Robert Harding Picture Library; page 45 - (left) Luiz Claudio Marigo, Bruce Coleman Limited, (middle) Terry Whittaker, FLPA, (right) Luiz Claudio Marigo, Bruce Coleman Limited.

Contents

How old is the Earth? 6
- How did the Earth form?

What is it like inside the Earth? 8
- What are the continents?
- How did islands form?

How are mountains made? 10
- Why are mountain tops often covered in snow?

What makes earthquakes happen? 12
- Can earthquakes happen under the sea?

Why do volcanoes erupt? 14
- What are geysers?

What are rocks made of? 16
- What are gemstones?
- Where do metals come from?
- What are iron and steel?
- What are fossils?
- What are fossil fuels?

How do rivers flow? 22
- What is a delta?
- Why do rivers meander?
- Why do waterfalls fall?
- Why are valleys different shapes?
- How fast can glaciers flow?

How are caves carved out underground? 28
- What are stalactites and stalagmites?

How do lakes form? 30
- What is the difference between a pond and a lake?

How much of the Earth is covered by sea? 32
- What is the difference between an ocean and a sea?
- How do waves form?
- What are tides?
- How deep is the sea?
- How salty is the sea?
- How do we get salt out of the sea?

How do coral reefs grow? 38
- What are coral atolls?

Why are the North and South Poles so cold? 40
- What are icebergs?

What are deserts? 42
- Are all deserts sandy?
- What are mirages?

Why do rainforests grow in the tropics? 44
- Why are the rainforests so important?

Glossary 46

Index 47

The meanings of the words in **bold** lettering in the text can be found in the Glossary on page 46.

How old is the Earth?

Scientists think that the Earth is about 4,600 million years old. The Earth was once a very different place from the planet we know today. It was covered in volcanoes, spitting out hot gases, rocks and **water vapour** into the air. As the Earth's surface cooled, the rocks hardened and formed the ground. The water vapour also cooled, then it **condensed** and fell as rain in violent thunderstorms. Some of the rain dried up on the hot surface. But some filled the first seas, which were almost boiling, and as **acidic** as vinegar. Instead of the oxygen we breathe today, the air was filled with poisonous gases such as carbon monoxide, ammonia, hydrogen sulphide and methane.

Scientists who study rocks are called geologists. In 1984, the oldest rocks so far known on our Earth were discovered by geologists in Canada. These rocks are over 3,960 million years old. The first living things were tiny cells that lived about 3,200 million years ago. The dinosaurs lived from about 200-65 million years ago, but our first ancestors did not appear until about 4 million years ago.

 Did you know?

The Earth is the only planet known to support life. This is because it has the right temperature and because the air is now fit for animals and people to breathe. But there may be life on other planets... what do you think?

The Earth would have looked very much like this 4,600 million years ago, before the first life appeared.

The planet closest to the Sun is Mercury. It is followed by Venus, Earth, Mars, Jupiter, Saturn, Uranus, Neptune and Pluto.

How did the Earth form?

The Earth is just a tiny speck in the Universe. This vast space contains billions of stars, planets and moons. Our part of the Universe is called the Solar System. It is made up of the planets and moons around our Sun. The nine planets are Mercury, Venus, Earth, Mars, Jupiter, Saturn, Uranus, Neptune and Pluto.

Astronomers are scientists who study the stars and planets. Most of them believe that the Universe began about 15,000 million years ago. There is thought to have been an explosion called the Big Bang. This threw clouds of hot gas and dust out into Space.

Astronomers think that the planets formed from these hot clouds, which were pulled together by the force of **gravity**. They also think that the Universe is still getting bigger, from the force of that same Big Bang.

This shows how a 16th century astronomer, Copernicus, saw the Earth and the Universe. He worked out that the Earth spun on its axis and around the Sun.

 Did you know?

The Earth measures 40,075 kilometres around the Equator, which is the fattest part of the Earth. It has a surface area of about 510,065,600 square kilometres. It is the third closest planet to the Sun, at a distance of about 150 million kilometres. The Earth's closest neighbour in Space is our Moon. It is about 384,400 kilometres away from the Earth. The diameter of the Earth is about 100 times smaller than the diameter of the Sun.

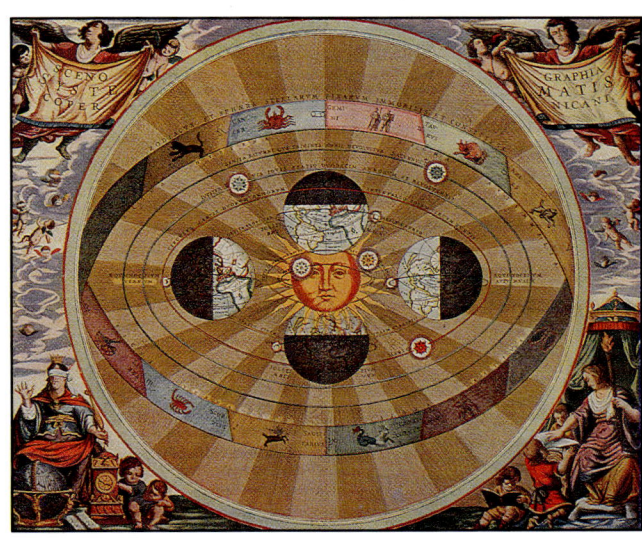

What is it like inside the Earth?

The ground beneath your feet is the outermost layer of the Earth, called the crust. It is made up of hard rock, covered in soil or water. The crust is about 40 kilometres thick on the continents but only about 8 kilometres thick on the sea bed. If you compare the depth of the crust with the overall size of the Earth, it is no thicker than the eggshell on an egg.

The crust floats on the next layer underneath it, which is called the mantle. Here the rocks are so hot that they are almost molten, or liquid. The mantle is about 2,900 kilometres thick.

The third layer is called the outer core of the Earth. It is about 2,200 kilometres thick. This layer is liquid as well, but it is made mostly of iron and nickel, which are metals. The liquid metals cover the Earth's core, which is a ball of solid nickel and iron about 2,500 kilometres wide. The temperature at the centre of the Earth is an amazing 4,500° C, but the pressure on the core is so great that the metals do not melt. Scientists have found out about these layers by studying the shock waves that shoot through the ground after an enormous underground explosion, such as an earthquake (see pages 12 and 13).

What are the continents?

The Earth's crust is not one single slab of rock. It is split into seven enormous chunks, and lots of smaller pieces. These are called plates. The large chunks form the continents – Asia, Africa, Australia, Europe, North America, South America and Antarctica. Which continent do you live on?

The continents have not always been in the same place as they are today. The chunks of crust on which they lie drift on top of the mantle below them. So they are constantly moving. About 250 million years ago, the continents were all joined together. They formed a huge 'super-continent', called Pangaea.

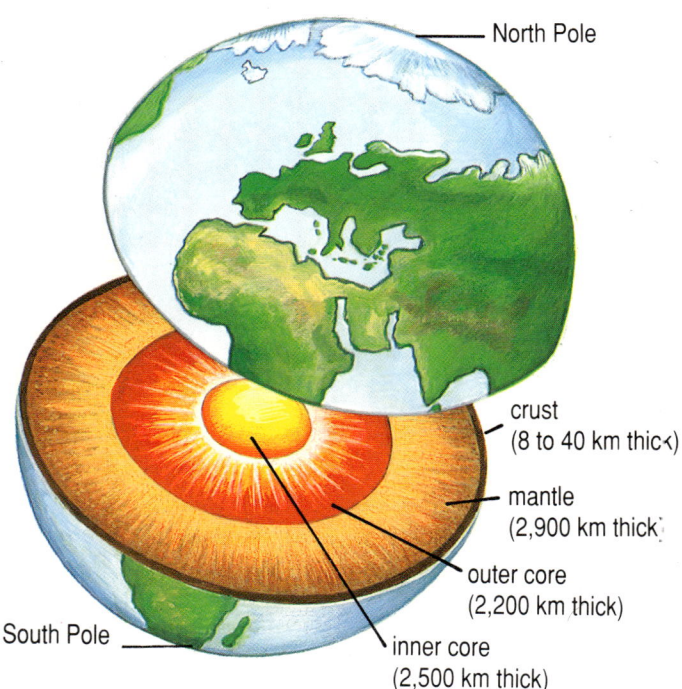

The Earth is made up of layers, a bit like the skins of an onion.

8

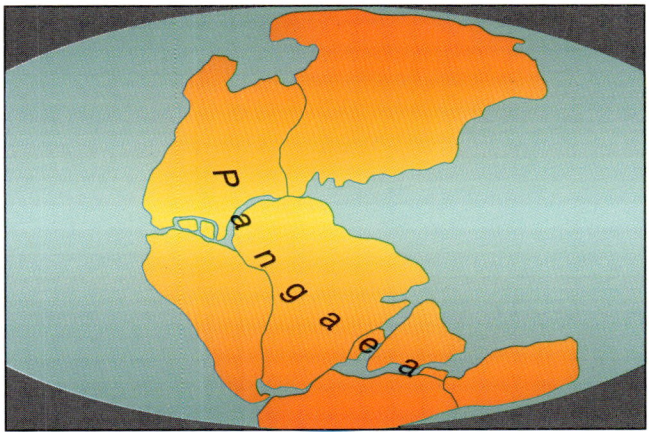
Pangaea.

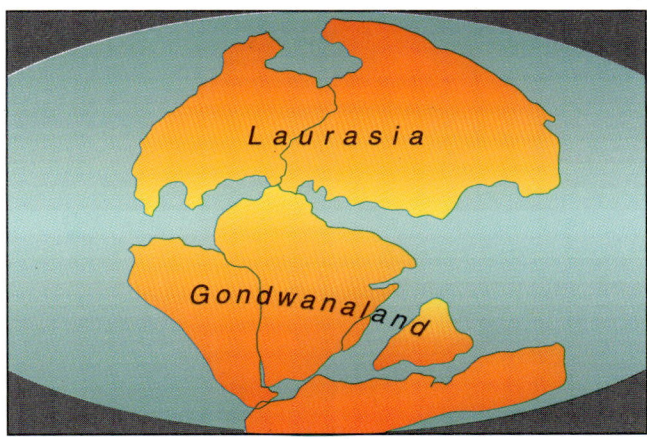
Laurasia and Gondwanaland.

Around it lay a vast ocean, called Panthalassa. About 200 million years ago, Pangaea began to crack up. At first it divided into two large pieces, called Laurasia and Gondwanaland. Then these two pieces began to split again into the continents that we know today, and they drifted into their present positions.

The continents are still drifting. Europe and North America are being pushed about 4 centimetres closer each year.

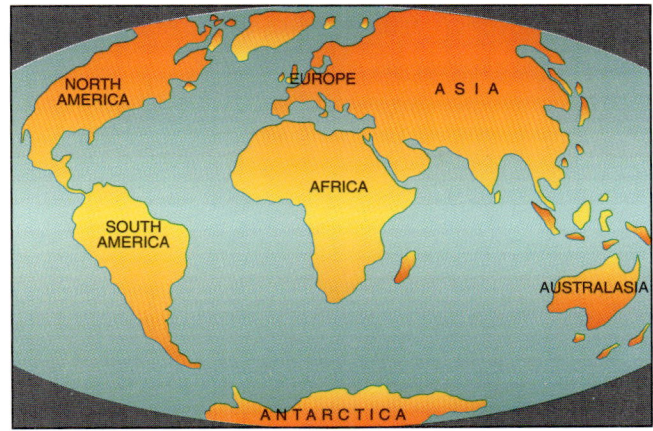
The continents as they are now.

How did islands form?

Islands are areas of land which are completely surrounded by water. Some islands lie on the smaller pieces of the Earth's crust. Others have broken off the continents. Madagascar, for example, was attached to Africa millions of years ago. It now lies about 400 kilometres off the south-east coast of Africa. There are some islands, such as the Hawaiian islands, which are really the tips of underwater volcanoes. Other islands are formed by volcanoes erupting underwater. Surtsey, off the coast of Iceland, erupted from the sea in 1963. The hundreds of tiny islands dotted about the Pacific and Indian Oceans are made from coral (see pages 38 and 39).

These two small islands are part of a long chain of coral islands called the Maldives. They lie in the Indian Ocean.

How are mountains made?

Some mountains are formed by volcanic eruptions (see page 14). But most are the result of movements of the Earth's crust. The rocky plates that make up the crust are always pulling apart or crashing into each other. There are two main types of mountain which are made by the shifting crust.

Fold mountains form when two plates crash into each other and the crust between them folds and crumples like paper. The Himalayas, the world's highest mountains, were formed like this at least 45 million years ago. The plate carrying India crashed into the plate carrying Asia, causing the sea floor between them to buckle up into mountains. Fossil seashells can still be found high up in the Himalayas.

Block mountains have flatter tops than fold mountains, and are formed in a different way. A huge block of rock is pushed up between two cracks in the Earth's crust. The Sierra Nevada range in the USA is a good example of this.

How a block mountain forms.

How a fold mountain forms.

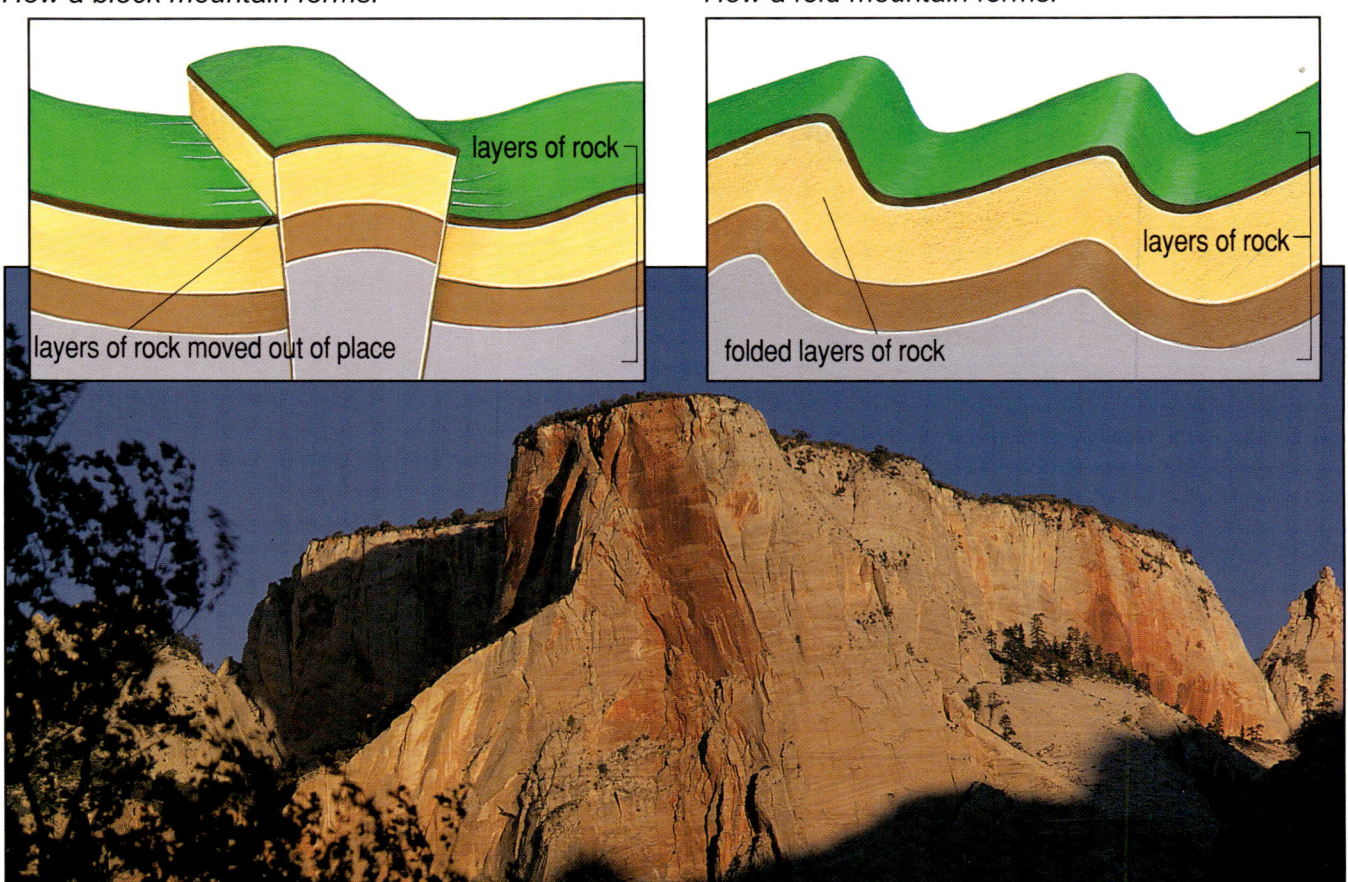

This huge rock in Zion National Park, Utah, USA, is part of the Wayatch Range. It is an example of a block mountain.

See for yourself

You can make your own fold mountains with four strips of plasticine. Arrange them in layers, one on top of the other. These layers are like the Earth's crust. Now hold your palms out flat and press against each of the ends of the plasticine. Your hands are acting as the colliding plates. As they push towards each other, they force the plasticine up into a mountain. You could try making a chain of mountains using longer pieces of plasticine. You may need to ask a friend to help push on one side.

Did you know?

Mount Everest in the Himalayas is the world's highest mountain. It is 8,848 metres high. The first people to climb to the top were Sir Edmund Hillary and Sherpa Tenzing Norgay in 1953.

Mount Everest in Nepal.

Why are mountain tops often covered in snow?

As you climb a mountain, you will notice that it gets colder. The temperature drops by about 1 °C for every 100 metres that you climb. This is why the tops of high mountains are often covered in snow, even though the **climate** may be much milder lower down. Some mountains, such as those in the Himalayas, are so high that the snow on their **summits** never melts. Mountaineers also have to cope with bitter winds and less oxygen than normal, so breathing is very difficult.

This is the Matterhorn in the Swiss Alps. Its pyramid shape was caused by erosion (see below).

Did you know?

Mountains are constantly being worn away by the wind, frost and ice. This process is called erosion. But it happens very slowly indeed. A mountain gets less than 9 centimetres shorter every 1,000 years.

11

What makes earthquakes happen?

Believe it or not, there are about 500,000 earthquakes every year. Only about 1,000 of these cause any damage, and only about 100,000 can be felt. The rest of the earthquakes make the ground shake so gently that no one notices them. But any **vibration** of the Earth's crust, however small it is, counts as an earthquake.

Earthquakes happen at the edges of the great plates of the Earth's crust. As two plates jostle and strain for position, they suddenly slip and slide. This causes the ground to shake. In the worst earthquakes, great cracks may open up in the ground and swallow up buildings, cars and even people. Most earthquakes last for less than a minute, but an earthquake in Alaska in 1964 lasted for seven minutes. Cracks 90 centimetres wide appeared in the ground.

As the plates move, shock waves shoot through the rocks in the Earth's crust. These are called seismic waves and they can be felt hundreds of kilometres away from the earthquake. Scientists known as seismologists, study these waves to find out more about the restless Earth.

The strength of an earthquake is measured on a special scale, called the Richter Scale. It goes from 1 to 10, and each number up the scale means that the earthquake is 30 times more powerful than the one before it. The worst earthquake so far measured 8.9 on the Richter Scale.

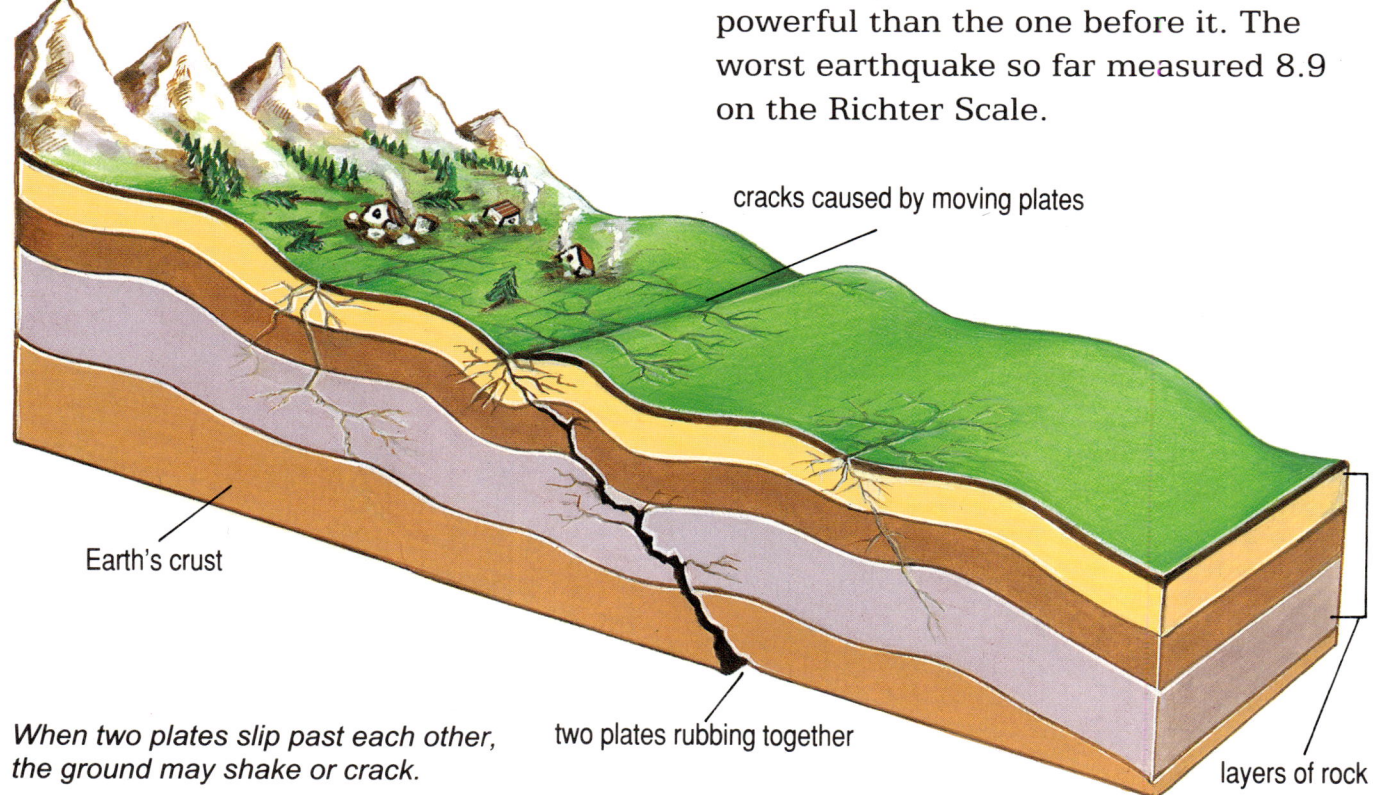

When two plates slip past each other, the ground may shake or crack.

Did you know?

In September 1985, a terrible earthquake destroyed large areas of Mexico City. Over 2,000 people died. The city's maternity hospital was knocked flat. But amazed rescuers later found 50 new-born babies who had survived under the rubble.

Above: Earthquake damage, California, USA.

Left: Mexico City, 1985.

Can earthquakes happen under the sea?

Many earthquakes happen under the sea and cannot be felt on land. They are known as seaquakes. The deepest happen about 750 kilometres below the surface. Very strong seaquakes can make ships shake violently. Others set off huge mudslides under the sea and can even snap underwater telephone cables.

Underwater earthquakes or volcanoes can also cause enormous waves, called tsunamis. These can speed over the sea and crash on to islands and coasts, drowning houses and people. The highest tsunami so far recorded was 85 metres high, taller than a twenty-storey building.

 Did you know?

About 90 per cent of all earthquakes happen in the area around the Pacific Ocean known as the Ring of Fire.

The Ring of Fire in the Pacific.

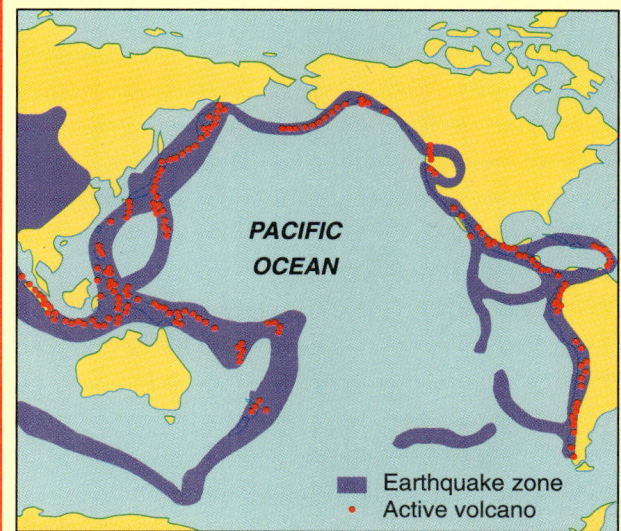

Why do volcanoes erupt?

An erupting volcano is one of the most dramatic sights on Earth. Deep under the Earth's crust lies a layer of red-hot liquid rock, called magma. A volcano erupts when pressure builds up underground and forces the magma up and out through cracks in the Earth's surface. After it has burst through the surface with rocks, dust and gases, the magma is called lava.

Volcanoes are different shapes, depending on how violently they erupt and the type of lava that pours out of them. Thick, sticky lava builds up a cone-shaped mountain as it cools quickly and hardens. Thin, runny lava flows much further before it cools and hardens. It forms low volcanoes, called shield volcanoes.

 Did you know?

Lava can flow at speeds of over 600 kilometres an hour. This is about twice as fast as an express train.

Lava is oozing out of this volcano in Hawaii, and flowing fast down the sides.

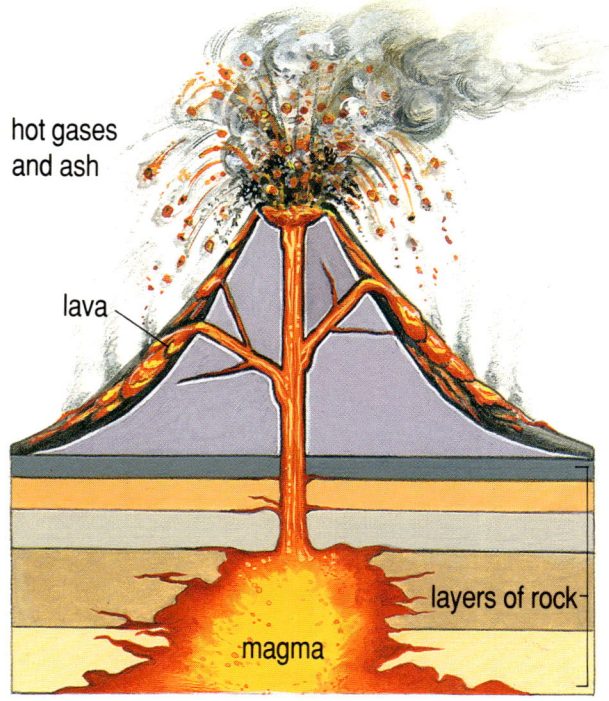

A cone volcano.

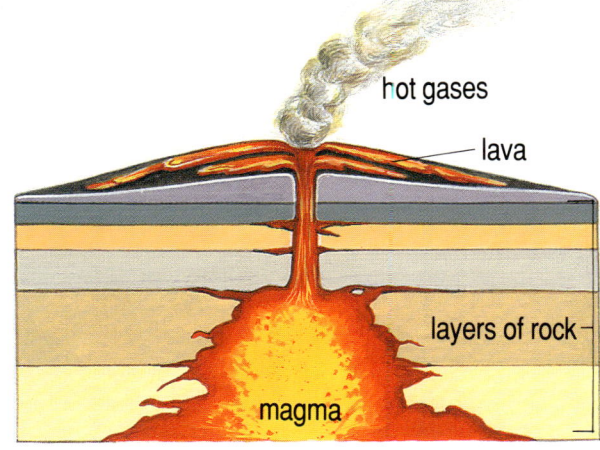

A shield volcano.

See for yourself

You can make your own working model of a volcano. You may need to ask an adult to help you. First, make a cone-shaped mountain out of sand or soil. Mix a teaspoon of baking soda (bicarbonate of soda) with some warm water in a test tube. Shake the tube so that the soda dissolves. Then add a few drops of washing-up liquid and a few drops of orange food colouring. Mix the ingredients together. This is your lava. Gently push the test tube down into your sand mountain. Now add a few teaspoonfuls of vinegar to the test tube until the mixture starts to bubble and fizz, and pours out down the sides of the volcano.

 Did you know?

There are about 10,000 geysers in Yellowstone National Park, USA. One of these is called Steamboat Geyser. It is the tallest active geyser in the world. It shoots up to a height of 115 metres.

What are geysers?

Geysers are fountains of scalding-hot water and steam which shoot out of the ground. They happen in places where there are lots of volcanoes, such as Iceland. The rocks under the ground are red hot. They heat any underground water until it is so hot that it bursts out of cracks in the ground.

The word 'geyser' comes from the Icelandic word, 'geysir', which means gusher. In Reykjavik, the capital of Iceland, hot water from geysers is pumped into people's homes and used in their central heating systems.

This geyser is shooting out hot water in Whakarewarewa, Rotorua, New Zealand.